I0173160

THE FINAL WORD…

Incoherent Ramblings from

————————

Matt Rouse

Huntington Beach, CA
Black Napkin Press
2016

THE FINAL WORD
Copyright © 2016 by Matt Rouse

32° Fahrenheit originally published by Culturedvultures.com

All rights reserved. No part of this book may be reproduced or transmitted in any form or by any means without written permission from the author.

ISBN-13: 978-0997446500
ISBN-10: 0997446501

Printed in the USA by Black Napkin Press

typewriter keys dance
to his poet's beat, rousing
fantasies to life - Graham Smith

Acknowledgements

To my editor Janet K Pyne: Thank you for taking this journey with me.

To my two muses: Lois and Bonnie, some day you will forgive me for this.

To the memory of Dennis Phillip Rouse, who didn't like my poetry because it didn't rhyme.

To Torrin for the poem that is too big for only one of us to write and has not at this moment ended.

To my family: the Burdicks, the Hulls, the Munces and the Pynes for your support and to Uncle George who has always been my biggest fan.

To Ben and Steve, the Two Idiots Peddling Poetry for giving me a place to hang out on Wednesdays.

Table of Contents

Dedication:

This collection is a result
of the encouragement of Susan Hull.
Please direct all hate mail to her.

THE TIME OUT TALES

Because the bunny
did not need a shave.

Because sticking the tops of the Yoplait yogurts
on the wall in a circle does not create a portal
to another universe.

Because calling your sister a "stinky buttface"
is not protected speech under the First Amendment.

Because leaving a trail of Jell-O from the kitchen to the bedroom
so you can find your way back is not an effective form of navigation.

Because hitting other kids over the head
with your lightsaber is a clear violation
of the Jedi code.

Because daddy's shampoo
is not a writing utensil.

Because peanut butter
is not glue.

Because you are not old enough
to drive daddy's car.

Because tossing spaghetti on the ceiling fan
is *not* artistic expression.

Because your school
is not clothing optional.

Because batteries
do not go up there.

Because your teacher
is not required to address you as
"her highness queen of the purple dinosaurs."

Because the remote control
is not a boomerang.

Because a water balloon fight
does not count as a shower.

Because the smart phone
is not a hockey puck.

Because you are not adopted.

Because hiding your milk box in your desk at school
is not an FDA approved method of making cottage cheese.

Because you can't un-friend daddy.

Because your sister's cowboy boot is not
a flower pot.

Because the neighbor's dog did not tell you
to emancipate it.

Because your middle finger
is not a windup toy.

Because we do not
eat with our feet.

Because hand sanitizer is not
your "happy sauce."

Because washing your dishes after dinner does not
violate child labor laws.

Because roller blades don't work
in the pool.

Because…
wipe when you're done with your business!

Because you are not
the reincarnation of the Buddha.

Because Daddy's book of poetry
is not toilet paper.

SEED

I found a seed
and brought it home
and planted it in a homemade, glazed ceramic pot
and put good soil around it
but it did not grow.

I watered it regularly and gave it plant food
I put it in the sun during the day
and in the house when it was cold at night
but it did not grow.

Every day I would come home from work and check on it
but it did not grow,
so I threw it in the front yard on the lawn
and forgot about it.

A month later
a little sprig of a tree had sprouted in the center of the grass.

I was looking at it when my neighbor stopped by

"When did you plant that oak tree?"

Two weeks later I received a notice from the landlord
that there was $100 charge
for unauthorized shade.

S'MORES

We spent the day in the water
body surfing in the shore break,
we shuffled our feet like the sign said,
so the rays wouldn't sting our ankles.
The kids sequestered themselves
inside a fort built out of beach towels and umbrellas,
but when the Barbeque Lays disappeared
the chips were rescued
and the castle was the razed.

Jeremy grilled burgers and hotdogs,
Tonya brought pineapple kabobs,
we cut the watermelon,
set the mustard upside down.
There was a Frisbee
and shovels,
a sand castle
with a moat.

When the day began to fade
we all gathered our chairs
as the reflection of the sun
setting behind the Catalina Isthmus,
off the white caps out from shore,
formed an arrow
that pointed right at us.
Clinton lit the logs in the fire pit.

It took a number of minutes
to position the chairs
so the ash and the exploding
sparks wouldn't hit us in the face.

The fire rose higher as
the sun sank away.
Julian brought out his guitar,
Dylan, and Lennon, and a little Jack Johnson.
Candice bought oversized marshmallows.
We impaled them with our metal spears.
Jim unwrapped the Hershey bars
someone had left them in the sun all day,
they were soft and got all over Jim's palms.
He joked that he looked like
he was going through the loop
at the main.

Bonnie insisted on
roasting her own marshmallow,
she grabbed it from my hand,
brought it close to her face,
smelled it,
licked it,
then jabbed it deep into the blaze.

I kept trying to lift the stake up,
but she kept putting it back
until the marshmallow was on fire.
Black and bubbling,
searing and popping.
She screamed in horror,
"My marshmallow's on the fire
it's burning
it's boiling,"
she raised it over her head,
swung it in the air wildly
like a villager chasing an abomination
running in place and howling

"Put it out daddy,
Put it out ,"
until Finally I grabbed her harpoon,
blew hard and ended the incendiaries.

I wiped the charred carcass
onto the graham cracker
atop the plasmic chocolate,
gave it to her and watched
as she sank into her
American flag folding chair
and destroyed the monster.

I slowly got up,
put another marshmallow on the spoke.
She grabbed it from me
and stuck it deep
into the heart of the flame,
I tried to lift it several times
but she always put it back.

The voices telling their tales
and the heat of the
glowing heart at the core of the fire
put me into a trace of remembrance.

12 years ago
I was begging for change
in front of a 7/11,
taking showers with a garden hose
or in the sprinklers.
Staggering through fog at midnight
in a self-hating haze
to the railroad tracks

behind the storage shed I lived in.

Every night I'd put
my head down on the rails
and wait for the train,
but it never came
fast enough.

Now I'm sitting in the
American flag folding chair
on the beach
around the bonfire at twilight,
the wind blows the smoke
from the blaze in rising spirals,
the kids lick the s'more guts
off their elbows,
the sodas are in the cooler,
the voices and the laughter
fill the salty air.
I lean over in my folding chair
and reach for a marshmallow.

DREAD PIRATE ROBERTS

The Dread Pirate Roberts
is and
isn't
an idea
a man
a man with an idea.

Disenchanted by the mainstream,
anti-government,
the ultimate capitalist,
economic anarchist,
binary cowboy.

An ancient warrior,
conquering the world
one city at a time,
until he marched his soldiers
down the Silk Road
and found himself
in an altered state.

Struggling to decipher
the encryptions of combat
the bits and pieces
of a enemy too large,
too advanced,
to evade.

Multi-national corporate spiders
lurch toward each other
on stealthy modern armored
saltpeter strands,

Dread Pirate Roberts
is frozen
stuck in the prison
of obsolete software
sentenced to a lifetime
of analog powerlessness.

One empty box of spent time
on top of another until
they fill the room.

Dread Pirate Roberts
is defeated.

Dread Pirate Roberts
will never be caught.

WAITING

Sometimes I feel that I'm not living at all,
I am in limbo,
in stasis,
immobilized,
I am outside my body staring at myself
standing still.

I am waiting.

I am waiting for a pay check,
for an apology,
for an epiphany,
I am waiting for the apoplexy epidemic
on the TV news to end.

I am waiting for
the next Kennedy,
the next Jordan,
the next king,
the next Einstein,
the next World War,
the next 911,
the next nuclear meltdown.
I am waiting for the next 7.1 earthquake
to hit a third world island country
so I can give 25 dollars to the Red Cross
and feel like a better person for a minute.

I am waiting for people to say what they mean,
I am waiting for people to not be so mean.
I am seventeen, it's my first job
and I am waiting tables on the night shift

at a French café called Mes Amis,
which means "with my friends" in French,
and the guy that runs it isn't friendly,
he gets drunk and yells at me.
I am waiting for him to choke on his snails,
I am waiting for the couple wearing too much cologne
to get done with their ratatouille
so I can collect my five bucks and go home.

I am waiting at the DMV,
I am waiting at supermarket,
I am waiting for a social security card,
I am waiting for service,
I am waiting in servitude,
I am waiting for a venti pike with room
and a blueberry cream cheese muffin,
I am waiting for my McGuffin,
for my presents,
for a presence,
for a precedent,
for the president to get spawned on
by a salmon while trying to talk
about climate change in Alaska.
I am waiting for Armageddon,
I am waiting for the apocalypse,
I am waiting for a reckoning,
a beckoning,
a bludgeoning,
a burning,
a barbecue.

I am waiting for a fascist dictator
to fire off a nuclear missile.
The next terrorist attack,
the next church shooting,
the next protest movement,
the next stock market crash,
I am waiting for civilized society to collapse so that
I don't have to pay taxes any more.

I am waiting for a revolution,
for a resolution,
for restitution,
for a revelation.
I am waiting for the second coming,
but feel that the kid from San Salvador
who works in the electrical shop
next to my office glows a little
and that I might of missed it.

I am wading through the sewers on Sunday,
I am wading through the shit they all flung back at me.
I am weighting down the bodies
with the memories of my transgressions.
I am waiting for the sea level to rise enough
to wash away the evidence,
the conspiracy,
the incidents,
the coincidence,
the co defendants,
your co-dependence .

I am waiting for my new halo,
for my Pulitzer,
for the applause,

for the laugh track to kick in.
I am waiting for all of you to recognize my genius.

I am waiting.

TIETA

Tieta the toucan got her beak ripped off
by a another bigger bird
while the two were locked in a small box
by animal smugglers
who were probably on their way to Tucson.

When she was rescued
in March
they said she was
tossing seeds and berries up in the air
with her lower beak,
trying to catch them with her gullet.
She only succeeded
in one out of five attempts

Scientists fitted her with a new beak
that they made from polymers
on a 3D printer.

It took two months to design her new beak.

It took two hours to print it.

It took two rivets per side to secure it.

It took two bottles of black nail polish to paint it.

She has trouble eating berries and seeds with it,
but she doesn't have any trouble with maggots
or cockroaches.

FRAGMENTS OF HER MIND

I saw it first thing in the morning on Monday
when I got out of my truck,
holding my blueberry pop tart and my coffee cup.
At first I thought the driver
had strayed too close to a city park
and got hit with a baseball
from an oversized 12 year old
trying to impress the
blonde girl with the pigtails
in the pink jersey playing soccer
on the next field over.

When I got inside there were three of them
standing around Trujillo's desk
across from mine
watching the data chip
from the onboard camera
mounted below the rearview mirror.

I did not go over and watch
but I could hear the sounds.
The sound of the driver talking
about how shitty being a cab driver is,
the sound of the passenger talking
about how shitty the weather in Minnesota is,
the sound of The Who on the radio,
the sound of a cell phone ringing,
the sound of the tires gliding over concrete,
the sound the driver suddenly cussing,
the sound of the passenger screaming,
the sound of the pedestrian grunting,
the sound of a human head meeting the windshield.

No one in the office could determine if it was our
fault or not,
but they all agreed the woman
was drunk.

After lunch I went out to the vending machine
to get a Dr Pepper
and saw the car in corner of the parking lot.
I walked up close,
the afternoon sun glinted
off hundreds rough edges of broken glass.
It appeared to me
a map of her neurons,
a shadow of her consciousness
flash burned in radial fractures,
her regrets pumping at light speed
through tiny cracks between angry shards,
pulsing in a winding web
up and down corridors of fissures.
The pain of recognition frozen
in semi concentric circles,
ruptures in thought,
pixilated in clear silicon.

I took my index finger and pushed it
into the depression.
It was elastic,
stretching past her reality,
downward in time
to the space right before
she walked across the street
without noticing the red light.

I let go with my finger,
inspected at the small fragments
glimmering at the tip of my thumb.

I saw in them a shattering awareness.
The recognition of something horrible,
something irreversible,
something yellow
coming right at her.

I went back inside,
tomorrow the window guy would come
and wipe the memory clean from cab 712.
I thought of her in the hospital
with a concussion,
would she remember?
Or is the memory lost,
left behind on the windshield,
synaptic fractures,
fragments of her mind?

THE SLAUGHTER OF THE DRAGONS

She's mad at me
because I killed her dragons.
Her lip is quivering,
her eyes water.
She says:
You killed all my baby dragons,
you erased my game
on your smart phone.

It was using too much data Lois,
this is a work phone.
No games.

She starts screaming:
Then get another phone,
one just for me.

I don't have money for that,
go get a job
and buy your own phone.

Five minutes later
she was still
sitting on the couch
staring straight ahead.

Then she turned to me:
How do I get a job?

BUCCANEER 3-6
in memory of Dennis P Rouse

I was on one side and Kristen was on the other
holding his hands
when he sucked that last labored breath in
and held it.
His eyes whitened and widened,
his mouth opened and
did not close.

There was a priest in the room
reading scriptures,
I don't remember which ones,
I don't know why he was there,
I guess it made us feel better.
Every one kept saying
that dad was going to heaven.
They didn't know him
like I did

He died in the same way that he lived,
in violent thrusts,
in vocal protest,
hitting on the nurses
and always planning his escape
from the ICU,
right up until the end.

On Friday I sat with Kristen,
dialed up Bill in London
and put him on speaker.

The three of us

along with Aunt Dianne
and Uncle Mitch,
made the decision
that we had been selfish,
and he would have pulled his own plug
a long time ago.

Three weeks ago I stood
in the doorway to his library
in the house on Granada
among the thousands of books he'd collected.
I looked at his green chair,
the sailing trophies,
and the model ships we built together.
The pictures of the grandkids,
the fish he caught that time in Mexico,
him in his uniform in Vietnam
101st airborne
Buccaneer 3-6.

Standing there in a quagmire
of the familiar and finality
I was rendered immobile
by an overriding thought

All
things
are
beginning
to
end.

I saw a copy of Carl Sagan's *Cosmos*
on the shelf in front of me.

Did you know that nebulas are exploded stars
and that stars are born in nebulas?

Monday night I took the kids
over to Mitch's,
they played pool
on the pool table
and pet the dogs
and chased the cats
and looked at the pictures
and ate the sandwiches
and drank some soda
and then we left.

As we pulled away
they saw the moon in the sky,
look at the moon
the little one said
It's so white and wide,
they call that a full moon.
There's a man in it

No,
that's not a man,
those are the craters,
they are holes
that form when the meteors
hit it.

No,
that's man.
He takes care of the moon.
He keeps it clean
so we can always see it.

DEDICATED RAT

For forty-two flights
I have taken these steps downward,
creeping backwards in spirals
on my way to the bottom floor.
Along the way I stumbled,
fumbled with the handrail,
but the next foot
doesn't hit solid ground
until after you take the step.
I do not know when or
where this staircase ends,
but I have counted the times
I got off on the wrong floor
and wandered through dim hallways
searching for an exit or some validation.
I have marked the doorways
I once opened in panic
without knocking
I have vowed never
to open them again.

The screams and the doors slammed
in my face
are scars I call wisdom.
The education I received
at a harsh university.
I can't tell you
how to get to where you're going,
but I can show you
the doors not to open.
Just don't be like me
and keep opening

the same wrong door
over and over.

Try some other doors.

I will trudge on,
a rat dragging a slice of pizza
to my secret tunnel.
I cannot give up now
I've come too far,
the climb is too high
to turn back now.

POETIGASM

A couple weeks ago I went to a poetry reading
for the first time in almost 15 years
and I read my stuff
and they read their stuff
and I thought that their stuff
was better than mine,
but someone came up after
and said that I had a distinct voice
and I thought maybe I do.

Everyone has a place
and I know right now what my place is:
You can write about love
and insomnia and trains and desire
and Monsanto and injustice
and the wage gap and colloquialisms
and fishing and cancer and the earth
and baking a poem and someone stealing your poems,
and I'll write about s'mores and the 99 Cent Store.
I'm the inconsequential poet,
the homogenized, pasteurized,
Disney-ified poet.
I'm the poet that makes you all look better,
with my stuff no one has to think too much,
no one is offended,
no one is disturbed.
You can warm your hands on my words
like a fireplace with a blizzard howling outside.

You see my problem is
that I'm shy and introverted,
I don't think I'm a good poet,

I don't think I'm good writer,
I don't think I'm a good person.
When I was thirteen
at the Baptist military school
and the teacher stood at the chalkboard
and wrote down all the stuff you do
to get into heaven
and all the stuff you do
to get into hell,
I decided that I was probably going to hell.

That I might not be the protagonist of this novel,
maybe I'm the villain:
The Vader,
The Voldemort,
The Dark Ventini,
The vegetated zombies
looking at your brain and
licking his lips.

I don't want to hurt anyone,
so I don't go out at all.
I just sit in my bedroom
with my door locked
and play Xbox
in my underwear,
and when I do see you
I try to say as little as possible,
but my insecurities leak out
the sides of our conversations
like tiny geysers of radioactive mist
lactating from the teats
at San Onofre.

Then I heard you that night
read your poems,
I went home
and I wrote with eyes closed,
without thinking about it,
when I stopped I couldn't sleep,
I laid in bed and stared at the ceiling.

When I heard it
the sound of her
syllables ,
she whispered her
pentameters
they resonated against my
alliterations.
I felt the plot points
on the inside of my allusions
stand
on
end.

She lowered herself
onto me and embraced my stanzas,
caressed my disorganized random fragments,
planted little wet kisses
up and down my loose endings,
rubbed my incoherencies,
tugged at my inconsistencies,
I grabbed her by the metaphors
slipped into her warm fleshy conceit,
we started rhyming in couplets
wrapping ourselves around the epiphanies,
thrusting in metered time
until in the rapture of the antithesis

I lose my enjambment
inside of her allegories.

At my laptop with my eyes closed
ejaculating stream of consciousness
that I'll make sense of later.
I did not write this,
it was conceived in a coupling outside of mind.
it was not constructed,
this is reproduction.

This is what my voice sounds like.

Everyone has a voice,
when you do not listen to it
it festers down deep inside of you,
rips apart your psyche
like a gremlin on the wing of the airplane,
slashing at the engines with his claws,
tearing out all the wiring.

Everyone has a voice,
it speaks in a tongue
that has no interpretation
for good or bad,
right or wrong,
birth or death,
time or space.

Everyone has a voice,
it is the bastard love child
of focus and insanity,
a climatic release
of emotion and experience,

pain and knowledge,
passion, compassion, anger, longing,
and life itself.

Everyone has a voice,
what does yours sound like?

INFLUENCES

I once read an excerpt
from Charles Bukowski's *Factotum*
at a poetry reading.

Afterwards my girlfriend said
that we needed to talk,
that Bukowski was
a misogynistic malcontent
and she couldn't date anyone
who liked Bukowski.

She broke up with me
I never saw her again.

I remember getting really depressed
that Bukowski was dead,
I wished that he was still alive
so that I could tell him about this.
He would have thought it was hilarious,
then he would have said
"Your poetry is shit!"

THE LAST NIHILIST
for RJ, Thomas and all who went to the Old School

Middle aged and balding with beer belly and
bad teeth,

he is fighting for a cause that died 20 years ago
when that Nirvana song played on the radio.

He believes in low art and freedom of expression.
In big shoes and dressing in all black.
In felt hats and Howard stern.
In cheap cigarettes and Friday night lobster buffets.

He travels around the world trying to climb on stage
at Iggy Pop concerts so he can tongue the old rock star
and take pictures.

He's an altruistic capitalist,
everybody gets some he gets the most.

He remembers the smells of the little club
in the corner of the strip mall,
sweat and whiskey and wet leather and

how it wasn't big enough for the all those people,
the floor sticky under his feet,
the band cussing and giving him the finger
before launching into a layer of white noise
which bored under his pores
to his growling bones.
The dissonance of amplifiers codifying the disaffection,
disenchantment, disappointment, disrespect,
into a laser beam of vitriol

that vibrated inside your teeth
and boiled your marrow
until your leukocytes steamed over and you had to move.
All the other punks felt it too
the grinding guitar pouring propellant into our skeletal systems
all our molecules de-stabilize like one hundred and fifty slingshots
loaded with ball bearings are pulled back at once and released
we are all propelled forward.

Loose projectiles
seeking targets,
armed explosives
detonating,
Forward lunging,
razor wired,
elbow cleavers
vacillating,
parabolic
decayed orbits.
Free electrons.
Base neutrinos.
In collision,
Hadron pulses.
Close bombardment.
Micro fissures.
Elemental
mass decaying,
carbon dated
bloody half-life
spitting buckshot.
Needled vice grips.
Bare brass knuckles.
Closed fist hand shakes.

When you view the mosh pit from aerial perspective
you can see low pressure weather patterns forming,
like a typhoon in the Philippines
or a Hurricane headed for the Coney Island coast.

He broke his foot at Rollins and got a concussion at the Vandals,
there wasa race war a Youth Brigade gig at the hole in Westminster.
He got hit in the head with a beer bottle when Hazel played.

Now when he drives his Prius down the street,
he sees a kid a red light with her Sub-humans jacket,
purple Mohawk, sixteen piercings, Beats by Dre
plugged into her Galaxy.

He wonders whether that means the movement
is dead or alive.
Is there a new generation?
Is there any left or is he the last nihilist?
Was he ever one to begin with?
Was there a movement, or was it just spontaneous release
of pent up sexual frustration
with a bass line?

OLD FISH
for Scott Burdick

Next to the big lake in the small village
tales were told of a many colored fish,
always hunted but never hooked,
who delighted in taunting the boats on the water
jumping high into the air
and splashing the fishers with his tail.
As time tore on, pictures were snapped
and t-shirts were sold,
all the latest tech and all the fancy spinners
failed to catch him.

Many years passed.

One day Old Fish cruised through the water
as he always had,
he saw specks of color floating by him,
he knew then that time was short

He sank sullen down to the bottom
and found a cave
where he stayed for many days.
He could hear the hooks drop
and see the sunlight reflect off of spinning metal
but he did not move.
He saw in his mind the sunrise over the mountains
and imagined himself leaping out of the water
as he had done day after day,
but he did not move

As the sun set on the third day
he saw a father and a child in a small boat

40

in the middle of the lake.
The father wanted to call it a day
but the child cried,
he had caught no fish.
Old Fish slowly flashed his dorsal and rose from his rest
closer to the surface he inched
and inched
until he could see a hot dog on a little pole
swaying in the water.

Old Fish swam next to it,
smelled it,
circled it.
He looked up through the water
at the shimmering sky.
He glanced down into the speckled blue
that passed into blackness below.

The father told the child to reel it in,
the child started to pull the line out of the water.
Flick struck fast,
he sunk his teeth into the hook
and pulled,
swimming as fast as he could the other way.
The child screamed and almost dropped the pole,
the father stood behind and helped
as Flick fought,
he tugged,
and he dove,
and he slashed
until the red of his gills fanned out from his flanks.

Finally Flick exploded out the water in a violent mass,
the child and his father brought Flick onto the deck.

Flick looked up at the sun for the last time,
he saw father and child staring smiling down on him.
Old Fish slapped his tail on the puddle of water
at the bottom of the boat and flicked twice
landing drops on both of their cheeks
then he lay still.
He felt the sting of air and welcomed
the oncoming abyss of eternity.

He was surprised and confused
when the child picked him up off the deck
and threw him back into the lake.

32 ° FAHRENHEIT

I walk carefully barefoot
with these loud noises in my brain.
I am not sorry we woke you,
their argument wasn't over.

I reach out with long arms
and clenched fists,
I cannot make any sense of it
the cold has made me numb.

I dig with both hands
into hard grey cement.
I am not worried about the thieves around me.
I have nothing left to take.

I push the green button
that ends the phone call,
I am bruised but not bleeding,
your thorns are blunt from overuse.

I take a drive along the beach
down a narrow ill-lighted road,
I hold no grudges in the aftermath
the fog here is so thick.

FIREBALL

We came from the reading
but the poetry didn't start until
we stopped talking.
The poetry didn't start
until I was lost like a nomad
in the labyrinth of the
student housing parking
and was drawn to the apartment
by Thomas's guitar playing,
like an ancient sailor
driven by a siren's song,
diving onto jagged rocks.
The poetry didn't start
till Donna and Taylor got there,
cause this party desperately needed
female energy.
The poetry didn't start
until Sanbud crashed in to it
like Mongol invasion,
sipping his poison slow and steady,
building his immunity,
riding his
Fireball!
Fireball,
ride that burn!

This is not a 50's B movie,
it's a 2015 Syfy channel movie.
The fight between the giant half crab
and the giant half avatar,
Fist beats slap,
foot slaps fist.

I declare you the victor.
The crab wins,
you beat the avatar.
Do you how hard it was
to remove from my happy trail?
I wish I didn't have to meditate to punk rock.
If I want to calm down,
I gotta throw in some Black Flag
But I can't focus on the
Fireball!
Fireball,
ride that burn!

In the red corner is
Iggy Izalia,
In the blue corner is
Nicki Minaj.
Clowns run down,
she's not classic SoCal.
Sometimes it fades into the background,
I wish Nicky rapped more.
I like Iggy better.
You need to leave.
Let's get ready to
Vogue
Vogue.
Let your body move
like a virgin prayer
on the borderline,
we stand alone—
together.
Yogis
meditating on the indecent Madonna,
and I'd do it with you

but I'm busy
in the center of the room,
with the laptop
on a barstool,
the delusional conductor
of a degenerate philharmonic,
sliding down a tone deaf
cacophony towards a
crescendo of
Fireball!
Fireball,
ride that burn!

Who taught you Swedish?
These are complex Kurosawa Sangria mysteries,
beer and liquor and quicker
and sicker,
and I'm boss hog,
and we're tearing up the couch cushions
searching for Sanbud's lost iPhone password
through Torrin's prismatic eyes.
Why does it feel like that ?
Why does it feel like last week
was a year ago?
Why I do I keep seeing
Fireball?
Fireball,
ride that burn!

DREW BARRYMORE: Welcome back to the
2016 republican presidential debate
I'm drew Barrymore and
our next question is for congressman
Voorhees. Sir what would you do with the homeless?

JASON VOORHEES: Kill them all.
DREW BARRYMORE: Governor Pinhead,
What would you do with the immigrants?
PINHEAD: I would impale them with hooks
and then I'd kill them all.
DREW BARRYMORE: Assemblyman Krueger,
What would your education policy be?
FREDDY KREUGER: I'd wait till they
fell asleep, then I'd kill them all.
DREW BARRYMORE: Senator Cruz
what would you do about gay marriage?
TED CRUZ: I'D KILL THEM ALL!!!!
DREW BARRYMORE: Thank you gentlemen
We will be back after this
Fireball!
Fireball,
ride that burn!

My schizophrenia is visual,
and hers is sonic,
I want to meet someone who smells
imaginary odors
and someone who
tastes hallucinatory food,
and then if we hooked up a girl
in a pink unitard
who felt spectral touches,
we have a schizoid Ultron
and we'd go out and
fight the reality,
and protect the planet
from the evil minions
of the vicious and insidious
Fireball!

Fireball,
ride that burn!

And as they round the final turn
at the holocaust sweepstakes,
its Underrated Asian Armageddon
in the lead, followed closely
by Turkish Denial.
rounding out the field is
Dresden Barbeque
Hors D' oeuvres at Idi Amin's
Syrian Pleasure Cruise,
and This Party.
As they head
down the stretch
it's nose to nose.
they're neck and neck,
it's too close to call,
it's a photo finish
and the winner is…
Fireball!
Fireball,
ride that burn!

In the last two months I have listened to 900 albums,
she chained the sun around her neck
he's drilled it into his knees,
and Paris is burning,
and screw you Taylor you know this story,
we'll come back to this when I'm drunk.
You need to drink faster.
Excuse me?
Excuse me?
Excuse me?

The beats and the bottle,
that's brandy and
I went to the bathroom after Donna.
How can such a nice girl
produce such a
Fireball!
Fireball,
ride that burn!

Muy Thai grappler Satanists
knocked out concrete pillars,
chained to the cancer.
Fifty shades of green in that poem.
I look better blurry.
In your skin.
In my skin.
Subliminal submission.
Read it,
write it,
speak in whispers at the counter,
a seduction of potato chips
and the body,
the temple,
the random ruin,
of Colbert talkin' about football.
Thomas back on guitar,
Aspirin maracas,
trash can, guitar back, chopstick,
beer bottle percussion.
A Sublime Pink Floyd Pixie lullaby
we sank back into our cubbyholes,
pulled the curtains closed,
we lit this black tread night with a match
I can smell the rubber wafting south.

I see the flames rise into the sky
in my rear view mirror
and the tendrils of smoke
stretch like needy fingers
all the way to the tips of the
Fireball!
Fireball,
ride that burn.

THE FINAL WORD…

Please don't stop talking
you are keeping alive right now.

Sitting in the comfortable chair
in the Little Sparrow,
you took the whole thing
and set it in front of us
and picked it apart,
piece by piece,
until the individual units
that made up the sum of the whole
were scattered across the table,
and you held each one up
to the light,
turned it slowly,
examining its measurements.
Consistency of form.
The recesses, ridges, rivets.
The imperfections.
The practicality of the applications.
Because you said that
if it does not satisfy,
it is not worth your time.

Don't stop talking now,
you're keeping me alive.

Attempts to kill a cockroach
with your entire body,
dancing in the street
to music whose words I do not understand.
The photograph of the human soul,
the mind in sepia ,
old black and white negative exposures
of the constant collective consciousness
conjugating the possibilities
the conjunction of probabilities.

Don't stop talking now,
you're keeping me alive.

It is comforting to
disagree with some one
vigorously without violence,
the thesis and the antithesis,
the photosynthesis of
fermented cherries.
This is the poem that
was too big for only
one of us to write,
the one that at this moment
does not have an ending.
This is the poem we wrote
in black ink
on a black napkin.
This is the exercise in futility.
This is the final word.

Please don't stop talking,
don't stop talking now,
you are all keeping me alive.

DEAR EDITOR

I sent you something today
that I want you to look at,
but it is not a piece of fiction.
I'd like you look it over very closely
and make sure it is clear
and has the right structure
and is consistent
and spelled correctly.

You're probably thinking
that I will do
what I have always done.
I will ask for your advice
and when you give it
I will say thank you
and ignore it.
But I have always
followed your advice.

Sometimes it takes a while
for it to sink in,
two years is my average.

Sometimes you have to
repeat it a few times
before I understand the severity of it.

There are some things
you've been telling me
for twenty years
that just now started
making sense.

Dear editor
Please let me know
if I am being pretentious,
contrite or self-serving,
if I have strayed off the point,
if I have played it safe
or gone too far,
if I have mixed my clichés
or blended my metaphors.

Dear editor
please let me know
if the fact that I put fire references
in a lot of my poetry disturbs you,
Or if is it comforting to know
that all I'm doing is writing about it
now?

Dear editor
Please don't be afraid to be merciless,
these poems are children,
they need guidance
or they'll runaround the page
and throw the concept
back at you like mud pies.

Dear editor
I did not intend to sexualize that.

Dear editor
I apologize for my phobia of punctuation.

Dear editor
No, it doesn't rhyme.

Dear editor
This poem will remain always unfinished.

Dear editor

About the Author

Matt Rause is a single father of two daughters living in Huntington Beach, California. He works in the transportation industry. After a long break from writing he has decided to get back into it. This collection represents his evolution from a hobbyist to a serious writer. He is eternally grateful to his friends and family who have encouraged this book that took 42 years to write.

www.ingramcontent.com/pod-product-compliance
Lightning Source LLC
Chambersburg PA
CBHW072036060426
42449CB00010BA/2293